Between Me and You

Ted Eames

for Jack

Special acknowledgement and thanks to: all members of the Borders Poetry Group past and present; the many and varied folk at the Shrewsbury Poetry Café; Liz Lefroy; Jack Eames; Carol Parr; Chris Parr; Alan and Daphne Eames; Kathy Biddulph; Royden and Nancy Josephson; Julia Koball; Maggie Taylor; Sue Hunt; Mike Spilberg; Rae MacBrayne; Kari Stevenson; Marjorie Forinton; Max Gorman; Neila Chrisp; Viv Peto; and all the current and future readers of www.maintenantman.wordpress.com

Between Me and You

Ted Eames

tedeames@btinternet.com

www.maintenantman.wordpress.com

©Ted Eames 2014

Published by Cairn Time Press, 73 Pyms Road, Wem, Shropshire, SY4 5UU

ISBN 978-0-9929510-0-9

Cover illustration: *Holding the Line* by Royden Josephson
(www.rdjosephson.com)

Printed by LeachPrint, 27 Nuffield Centrum, Abingdon, Oxon, OX14 1RL
Tel 01235 520444
www.leachprint.co.uk

Contents

Between

Terminal.
It's a strange word for a jumping off point,
a portal into Between.
Between is a happy place to be.
What happens in Between
stays in Between.
It has had a bad press,
but Between is a fine place to talk, to listen,
to hear confession and to confess.
There are fewer rules in Between;
conversations cut quickly to the truth,
and knowledge, for once,
beats information.
The ferry, the bridge,
the border, the threshold:
liminal beings one and all –
though the ferry is closest
to the sublime spark gap,
the vault of the current
from pole to pole,
from shore to shore,
from one to other.
Between is where words in brackets
outweigh the rest of the sentence.
It's a good word for the enclosure of connection.
Terminal.

Moonstruck

On her slick-liquored back
in the bubblewrap
bladderwrack, her late evening
sunset-drowsy eyes
invite me in, in
for warm, salt-honey juice –
secret succulence
amongst the slithery greens,
the slippery chromes
of the sea-rank clots of kelp.
Heart-pulse ripples of water
and of rhythmic sound waves
from distant rock-broken breakers
lap our silver-oiled skin.
We roll in fleshy cadence,
bursting wet briny breath
from the heat-pressed, swollen
pods of our seaweed nest.

Charming, fey-but-coy, wistful:
mermaids have been censored
into garden-safe disneyed sprites –
but she was all abawd lustrous
lickering, suckling voluptuary,
all sensuous moonlit motion.
Gouts of moist film thick-coat
the silken scales that glisten
the weigh to her tender
plashy pleasure.

The Iron Filing, the Flock Flying,
the Human Being

Matt grey hundreds-and-thousands,
tiny cylindrical poppy seeds,
the carbon-dark iron filings
attract and repel into fine line ferns
from the magnet's unseen suck and blow.

Loded with longing, each black dot
within the wheeling, thrilling bird throng
hugs the pure, obscure, shifting symmetry
of tugging current and polar obligation,
obeying the soaring grace of ebb and flow.

Desire rules our own generous sweeps,
each patterned nuance of our traces.
Drawing closer is simultaneous pushing away
in the magnetic dialectic of the unlike and the like.

What We Discovered On Our Journey - 1

We came across a waterfall
and called it Beautiful Chance,
for subtle, casual calibration
of river flow, height of rock face,
balance of cool and warm,
all conspired that day
to mist the tumbling droplets
into steams of vapour
an air-fathom above
the ripple-free, untroubled
skin of the pool below.
Slowly, inevitably, the bead-cloud
rose back upwards,
condensing on the lips
of the cascade tumble-brink,
eager to plunge again but rise,
never touching fall's end –
a cycle of moving and being.
On another day a dry cliff
or a thunderous boiling
of seething coconut-white .
But that day, Beautiful Chance,
we witnessed our own
circular passage: from
parting to return, loss
to gain, descent to ascent.

What We Discovered On Our Journey (2)

The coming of the ice has planed this plateau's lake to frosted glass,
shamfering the shoreline fringes to limb-stumps of dun driftwood,
stark and stiffened with such chill loss of wave-washed motion.
Thickening panes at our feet lattice glossy brown twigs
and screen freeze-frame mopheads of yellowed grass.
Where can we pick a path through this frozen desert,
how may we read the blue sweeps of cold contour
crossing this hacked-into-the-horizon gelid plain?
The glacial sky is just as rime-schemed, fixed,
mirror-frozen, a petroglyph in a stone lake:
in this map we find slush beneath clouds
and hard, trusty footing under ether.
We navigate by this shifting chart
for one whole bright starless day,
arrive, safely, on chosen shore.
Now one among us must
seed a story, a tale
to be grown here,
to crystal-shape
this learning
blueprint.

After the Muddy Watershed

I found you when my sister broke her arm,
Mum and Dad at the hospital —
late night (black 'n white) telly worked its charm.
Pulsing swagger-music of a throbbing vein
vain man all shiny black and sweat polished
lop-sided smiling nodding at the very definition
of insouciant whatever that means to muddy floody
waters with his bias-in-the-bowl face all Cherokee
and slave ancestor featured braggart with back-up
all sexual braggadocio rhythmic twelve bar
throbbing vein of the erectile clitoral phallic nipple
stinging electric strut of such guitar confidence
and that knowing winking noble muddy bloody
waters face and glistening arch-brow challenge
cascaded through me that night of brimful blues.
You found me when my sister broke her arm,
big brother let me stay up —
late night (black 'n white) telly worked its charm.

Passion Wears No Slippers

I love it when you cootch up close to me
but your comfort zone is drifting away
inside some brittling browning plastic bag
snaggled up in the topmost branches of a wintry tree.
I love it when we are in the same room
but my comfort zone is stumbling lost
across some tussocky tundra waste in Siberia
benumbed bedraggled and benighted.
I am here to speak ill of the comfort zone.
[The comfort zone's a fine and private park
But none, I think, do there enjoy the spark.]
Cootch up now across that glint-gap
until we redefine both zone and comfort.

Cajun Night at The Guildhall

Tonight we are merely a two-step from heaven
as the accordion choreographs our votive shuffles.
'Louisiana Chanky-Chank' the afficionados call it.
Here in the Guildhall, all panelling and heraldic device,
it's more a case of Lichfield Chunky-Chunk
as marbled slabs of matronly flesh
rhythm-jerk in time with stubbly beer-bellies,
and short pink denim-splitters
perform swaying coital spasms
with tall ex-Rubens models.

Now the band squeezes, saws and strums,
metallic with chain-mail washboard and tingling triangle
as medieval banners stir in the warm air
rising, step by feverish step,
from sweat-darkened check-shirt and pale blouse.
Jambalaya, craw-fish pie on the Bayeux !

Couples twirl, couples step and re-step,
all in a tight, pre-set, pre-paired routine,
as if trapped in a back and forth film loop.
The best bring a heart of Saturday night to it all,
making a spastic, incontinent coming of their marking-time.
And, yes, it is all about couples,
and about repeated comfort of motion,
mature hetero hand in mature hetero hand,
two-by-twoing it toe-to-toe
till these fine Middle Ages floorboards
out-solo the relentless fiddle.

'Nuit Cajun' the posters declare.
This hall rather proclaims tales of Knights and Wives of Bath,
a skipping pilgrimage to a very Midlands mid-life Bayou.

The Marriage of Equals

They first met when both were aged 7
but by the time she was 15
he was still only 12,
and when she was 19
he had barely reached 14.
Now, was it some single great leap
or did he just speed up?
Did he jump
or was he pushed?
For when she hit 27
he was marking 40
and when she passed 40
he was at least 61.
As she celebrated being 52
his birthday cake candles numbered 85.
Of course,
they were no longer together by then.

Bye, Mum. Bye, Dad.

'Ring us, please, when you get home
just to let us know you're safe and sound'
stood for decades as your parting refrain,
a ritual nod to ties of blood and common ground.

The perils of the journey now behind me
I would pick up the phone on closing the door –
I could sort myself out, relax, unwind the road
as soon as I'd performed this empty family chore.

If you were dead I could pretend
that you might care enough to still require
my reassurance that I had survived the miles
and had not fallen prey to earth, water, air or fire.

But in your gathering painful numbness,
your farewells no longer make that small request.
How my heart beats for you to ask me this again,
as if your child's safety might help you rest.

The Lord's Care

Our children, which art in London,

Lasting be thy Power of Attorney.

Thy wisdom come.

Thy decision be done in care home

As it is in hospital.

Give us this day our daily bread

(but let it not be a ham-sliver sandwich made with thin-sliced white bread that has soaked up the water from the lichen-like lettuce leaf that has been tossed onto the plate in an alzheimer echo of healthy eating).

And forgive us our trespasses

(out onto the busy main road to get away from widescreen eardrumming daytime tv and bland pictures on the bland walls that seem to have been culled from some dingy b 'n b in the early 1950s, where both b's stand for bland, and safe cosy sing-songs and endless hours of toothless gibbering and soul-biting silence)

As we forgive them that trespass against us

(by ignoring the excrement that someone has smeared on the lounge wall in a final tragic act not of protest but of grouting, and by smirking at our loins, and by fucking well patronising us at every fucking opportunity).

And lead us not into temptation

(to write something or paint something or draw something or read something or listen to something or sew something or sculpt something or save something or surprise someone with something or laugh at something or get angry about something or touch ourselves where we remember it's nice to feel touch).

But deliver us from evil

(by letting us choose to die).

For thine is the wisdom,

The Power and the Attorney

For ever and ever.

Amen.

Visiting Hour

I.
Glimpsing her languid tongue,
and gentle with her folds of paper skin,
I feather this neat grooming-razor
across my mother's chicken slack jowls,
chin, upper lip, wick-and-tallow neck.

Some infernal life-preserving drug
is forcing thickets of silver filament
from her fear-becalmed face;
I must re-enact this tender shaving
perhaps three weeks from today.

If necessary.

II.
Before setting out
I selected a brand new battery
to ensure a true swift whirr.
Long-life's double-edged alliteration,
old-gold and black,
childhood charged with Wolves' colours
of my Molyneux afternoons,
a mother's rest time
from my restless mind.

III.
We sprinkle lavender
about her hospital pillows
that she might sleep,
though not yet deep enough.
The purple label
on the vial
perfumes another memory,

the only time I saw her joyful,
excited, full of hope.
Our first council house.
I was four and she sat me
on the painted concrete floor,
and we gorged on sweet tarts
with lilac icing with
deeper mauve scented
hundreds-and-thousands.

IV.
Without touching her waned flesh,
her sputtering waxen veins,
I strive to trim the bristles close.
She looks better for this
as drowsing steals across her.
She feels better
(I tell myself).
Some inner guttering flame
warms her jaws apart,
searching out oxygen morsels.
I see her tongue loll
lax behind her lower gums.
Release is a swallow away.

Should I tell nurse?

Up There

Our father,
What is it that you see on the ceiling?
You are unmistakably looking at...
at what? Not the broad bland insulation panels,
vacant sheathing for bellyful entrails of ducts,
guts and cables, intestines and wiry vein-cords –
the hospital's own finite life support system.
We stroke the shiny cell skein of skin, stretched,
a clinging cellophane film, across your temples –
but your eyes remain rolled upwards, misted now
with the grey-green gloss of a pigeon's sheen and
fixed on some makeshift screen, some shadow-play
archival footage that transports you, fills you
with wonder and calm and hope – a baby
suckle-riveted to a vision of the nearby breast.

What do you see on the ceiling, Dad?
The answer is sealed and unreachable,
an infinity away from the tumble of images
that cascade from tins and albums as we
clear your cooling, stiffening, dying home.
Memory is an over-rated asset in the end –
flakes of fact that cannot survive earth or air,
let alone fire and water.
At the death, inner vision is all.

A Tree Is Born

Surely you did not grow?
You were shoved, violently rammed upwards
into the not-tree air, after full forming
in five times five fathoms of earth.
Yes, your leaves have grown,
perhaps your smaller, fresher twigs –
but that granite trunk?
Those thunder-thigh branches?
That stone-sculpture bole?

No, you were perfectly hidden,
veiny root system and all,
soil-smothered and waiting,
poised for that astonishing up heaval,
that heaving up by giant hands.

With a shuddering shower,
a wet dog thrashing of brashing,
all earth, fibres, loam and grit,
you emerged complete, confident,
ready to be seen, no adjustments
beyond a little shaking and sprucing.

Now you state symmetry to the sky,
such a pre-formed wholeness
to shock our senses
with such massive presence.
Now you can bud and burgeon,
get on with the Spring leaf job
and the Autumn shedding task.

From now on all is slow calm
compared to the sudden power
of your immaculate conception.

I Crawl, You Caw

Rib me, rag raven, razor eyed
black laser dyed
carbon claw-print
on hard ash flint.

Mock my white knuckle rock-face stance
show off your prance,
spring-heeled crag hop
dance on stone-crop.

Pointedly, your jet-thatched coal beak
labels me weak.
Take flight! Swoop! Soar!
Crow in my craw!

Someone Is Watching Over Me

Lammergeier leaves the lasered bones,
lancet beak honed on calcium laminate,
calcarine grapple-clasp claws grasping at gravel.
I have startled a fibre-stripper,
a neb-wielding shred-peeler
completing a clean carcass-cage
for the bleaching blanching sun.
The wide feather-frame kite wings beat their whump,
needing all four syllables to lighten the ground:
lam-
mer-
gei-
er;
and the air now wears the weight,
gives warm coasting currency
to an unhurried gloating glide,
gleam-eyed, unhungry but greedy,
Braille-reading the land's every goose bump
with a drifting finger of shadow,
always ready for fresh-dead red flesh.
Lammergeier is browsing my trail.

Cairn Time

We have reached up, and now we are here,
circling this sack-dump of rocks on a hard place.
The stones of the cairn summarise our steps,
concentrate our senses,
compress our energy
into wide-base compact cone.

Cairn-time is different, special –
a spell cast from attainment,
relief, nourishment, desire.
We are alive for every degree
of the three hundred and sixty
that radiate from our being.

Sometimes we can linger lovingly,
sometimes the elements blast us away,
sometimes we are cold-numbed
into urgent movement down.
But we carry the memory of each summit space,
that moment when our hearts steadied.

A Book at Bedtime – the Haiku Years

No matter how hot
the bed – the wet patch becomes
all too quickly chilled.

No matter how cold
the wet patch – our warm desire
will soon restore heat.

No matter how hot
the bed – the wet patch becomes
all too quickly chilled.

No matter how cold
the wet patch – our warm desire
will soon restore heat.

To be continued,
the verses alternating
till bed is for sleep.

The Demiurgent Message

By their creation myths shall ye know them.
Tell us the healthy gendered stories
about the giants and the Earth Mothers,
all the morning sickness,
seed-spilling and splitting of wholeness,
the lightning bolts, the umbilical cords,
the bears, tigers, ravens, loons, hordes
of golden frogs and sea-turtle packs,
the collision of sky and ocean,
the Eggs and the eagles,
all the variations on the binary
yins and yangs
and twins and Bangs,
the Way, the Chaos, the Desire,
the lick of ice, the bite of fire,
the sparks across the great cow's teats,
the hermaphroditic feats,
the Word, the sacred druid
waving from primordial fluid,
the pregnant bumps and
lactating breasts,
the sweat droplets
of a supreme formless entity,
the weeping of copious fertile tears
and the underwater world seers,
the hyena, coyote and snow-white goose,
slippery salmon in vaginal juice,
the shells, the wolves, the lotus flowers,
the boats and winds and Life-Tree towers,
all the navels, mud and dreams,
copulations, separations. Tell us these tales!
Only one tradition makes woman the weak betrayer.
By their creation myths shall ye know them.

Time Runs In, Time Runs Out, It's the Bit In the Middle We Care About.

Three minutes will be all it takes,
the flurries of the boxers' round,
no matter all the taps and shakes,
the grains will find their own pace down.
The egg-shaped glass may work a treat
but cannot stretch to time's wide range.
Inflating ends would be so sweet
and sharpen up the sand exchange.

Moment by moment our dear past increases
and moment by moment our prized future shrinks.
Hour by hour tomorrow decreases
whilst from each bright second, tight yesterday drinks.
So seize NOW by the waist, but sorry to trouble you,
the 'N' will be dead by the time I write 'W'.

The Villainous Couplet

The Villainous Couplet held sway for years,
It made English Lit a dull vale of tears,
All smoothness, polish and spurious wit,
Superficial charm was part of the kit.
Tum titty tum titty tum titty tum:
Forget subtle language, just use a drum.
What is 'heroic' in such endeavour,
When poetic pride is so clever-clever?
Couplets are soothing, couplets are silky,
Pleasing to those who like their sops milky.
For sure there is craft in the usage of rhyme
And it serves poets well time after time,
But form can be tyranny all too oft
When meaning's below and technique's aloft.
Poetry's good name – such daylight robbery –
Has yet to recover from heroic snobbery.
Thank you Romantics, and thank you T.S.,
You helped get us out of this straitjacket mess,
We've broken our chains, with verse blank and free,
No longer bound by the stiff or the twee.
The craft's still demanding, harder in fact
Than painting by numbers a new couplet tract!
Roses are red and violets are blue,
It helps to be glib in this Heroic stew.
Heroics are fine when driving satire,
So stop now, Ted, you've just got a flat tyre.

The Happy Tamper

"I may be a digger
but I'm not very grave!"
is his line of choice
when people ask his living.
You know he's right
when earthy chuckling
accompanies each steady
legs-then-torso disappearance.
"Say what you like
about that Fred West",
he gasps mid-spadeful,
"but he were a grafter!"
A cheery, disrespecting song
until he is just a head,
like an obliging Dad in the sand,
or a sweating, Apache'd cowboy
waiting for angry ants,
till he's only a bobbing scalp
as the sixth foot is flung up and out,
soft muscovado loam to sweeten
the grievers' token fistfuls
knocking on the coffin door.

He likes his next bit best,
the tamping and the stamping.
He reappears slowly, evenly,
rising on a rectangle of packed soil,
his iron, flat-base, Great Leveller
thumping his mate's shovelled loads.
"It's Florida for me holidays",
he confides to the peace-seeker
trampled beneath his sole.
Imagining a polite "Which part?"
he punches out "Tampa!"
with a satisfied grunt
for each punishing syllable.
And as he spade-twins
yet another turning worm:
"That's made two of 'em
to chew your guts now!
I'm for cremation, me!"

Nothing Like the Real Thing

We knew all the steps then mistimed the motion.

...the coming was real
but the loving was fake...

We saw the bright tarns but never the ocean.

...your coming was real
but your loving was fake...

We tasted sweet honey but lost the whole hive.

...my coming was real
but my loving was fake...

We heard the directions but failed to arrive.

...your coming was real
but my loving was fake...

We scented the petals but missed the full flowers.

...my coming was real
but your loving was fake...

We touched for swift seconds but wasted long hours.

...the coming was real
but the loving was fake.

A Hare in the Mountains

One alert touch of a singular energy
tingles the collar of my boot
as tough pad flat back feet
startle my wakeful doze,
golden fatigue gift from
the red-eyed midnight sun.
Beside my prone form
a tight single sinew
squats all ready-steady,
one taut muscle with dark eyes,
a cocked crossbow of a hare.
The mere focus of my glance
triggers a starter pistol
in the crackling air between us;
the throbbing tendon untenses,
snaps like a sheet in the wind
and lithes away, springing
a crazy-pave hopscotch;
a merely half-sane path
sprinters the alarmed rocks.

Shoreline Meeting

Wet cat ?
How wild ?
Slinking as if stalking.
Your eye looks back at mine,
and that is no eye of cat
in your gleaming head.

Only drowned cats are that drench-wet.

You proclaim otter
as you wriggle the rocks
to confound my stare.

You are sodden clay,
glistening from slapped water,
fur-lines chiselled in mud-furrows.

For a moment you are more solid than wild cat,
then you are not drowning in sea-rings,
a liquorice spine among floating weed.

Truth in the corner of my eye
has flickered by before,
but such a direct gaze
drives me from the shore.

This look from other
grants me thrilling fear.

"Sorry, Mate, You Can't Come In!"

I know you're in there somewhere,
horseshoe ridge walk to conical peak.
I know you're up there in the clouds
by the sardined, finger-print whorls
of the map's fine brown contour lines
(time-out guide to What's On in the hills today).
Yet here we huddle, weathered, isobarred
by this burly, hurly security firm of a storm –
such a thick-necked bouncer of rain,
such a knuckle-duster bruising of hail,
such a shaven-cropped bully of gale.

Suit bulging with muscular torrents,
this squall of a doorman enforces "No entry –
no leather trainers, no fleece ties, no goretex jeans!"

Ullapool, I Won't Be Long

Moving near to you from the south,
always seems blessed with golden sun,
all pink gloaming rocks and life glowing trees.
This is the leaf's last party
before growing tough, exotic, rare.

Moving towards you from the north
is memoried with mist and rain.
broad, profound browns and greens
shallowed, narrowed by dull grey wash,
hiding a land where stark and subtle reconcile.

From the south we are about to enjoy you,
your catch-in-the-breath look of lochans.
From the north we are about to leave you,
to exchange hill-track for tarmac,
white-sanded bays for work-branded days.

From the south I pass through your streets
on my heart-leaping way to being mended.
From the north I linger in your comforts
on my way to becoming broken again.
Again you remind me that I am not from here.

In that reminder lies your healing, hurting truth –
you guard the approaches to a place
that gouges and grooves a line so simple,
so rich, so austere, so whole-making:
nobody belongs anywhere, place does not care.

O.M.G.

Dear Lord
I humbly pray that one fine day
you will find it in your heart
to become Christian, Jew or Muslim –
a non-fundamentalist version of any
would feel like progress.
Become a Hindu by all means,
or better still a Buddhist
(they kill many fewer than the others).

I humbly pray that one fine day
religion may become your gateway
to acquiring a little morality,
to accepting some responsibility
instead of blaming it all on us.
The good? "I made it all in seven days."
The bad? "Humans chose to invent it."
The ugly? "Don't talk to me about Dawkins."

I humbly pray that one fine day
you will learn Omniscience
means little if not applied in action:
you can in deed intervene.
And your vaunted Omnipotence
means you have the power
to please phosphor-frying children
as well as the comfortably converted.

I humbly pray that one fine day
you will become sufficiently Almighty
to shake off that nagging,
persistent personification -
the superglue male pronoun.
Perhaps on that day it may also come to pass
that you will cease to be humiliated
by your most embarrassing creation:
the Creationist.

I humbly pray that one fine day
you'll be just another word in our Roget.

Return Ticket

A treat-trip in childhood: bus to Wellington,
train to Wolves High Level, walk to Wolves Low Level,
train to New Street, kohl colliery of a station
darker than paleo-Lascaux, and with coarser graffiti.
Senses keened by rarity of leaving Shropshire
(oh pity the daily commuter's jaded eye)
I gazed down every busy detail of seething industry
corrugate jungle-packed on both sides of our track,
dense concentrate of manufacture, metal making,
machine moulding, pressing, turning, hammering:
glowing glimpses of the molten, a confidence
of crafted focus amid the teeming, tight tumult;
a twenty minute ride of gawping Pathé privilege
through raw, grime-prosperous human energy.

Today, though High and Low have compromised
on Wolverhampton Mean, the line to New Street's pit
drills only through strata of cold rust, blackened brick.
Ghosts of Pride Past scavenge the few new works,
semi-regenerated, stalled facades to mirror
the gutted, tottering cell-combs of silenced hives.
A pittance has been lavished for the old canals –
toehold towpaths for slow junkies and fast joggers.
Hermetic yards, archway roofs fenced and barbed,
abandoned workshops scalped to the flaccid rain:
all are Cornell boxes mulched of broken glass, buddleia,
crevassed rubber, tough tussocks, corroded iron.
In each trackside enclave, the unopenable windows
of my grown-up carriage frame a riveting entropy.

nevelE eniN : kroY weN

Thick clouds of dust, dove-grey, recede;
wither backwards as if ogre-sucked
from the swiftly brightening streets.
Here, hundreds of sweating citizens
run madly in a desperate reverse charge,
chasing the shrinking billows of pale soot
down concrete boulevards and shadowed alleyways,
until these citizens can slow to a walk
whilst the chalky cumuli ravel inexorably
up two rapidly engorging, rising towers
until they meet fierce flames in the upper storeys.
Tiny human figures, prone and pulverised, fill with bone again,
zoom plumb-line upwards as if on wires
from reassembling pavements – vanishing noiselessly
into high windows that mirror an indifferent sky.
Now the fires are quenched by condensing dust and debris,
till a lumbering, droning passenger jet backs smoothly
from each quickly pristine tower, a slick withdrawing
that leaves no mark, no threat, no sign of danger.
Inside each shiny aeroplane, purposeful men
squeeze backwards into aisle seats and rehearse
careful plans amidst dreams of heavenly reward.

Meanwhile in Gaza, and on the West Bank
tanks grind only onwards, jets strafe only forward.
True relentlessness defeats all wishful thinking.

Katy Jurado Speaks: No It's Not All Quiet on the Western Front

Tex-Mex sex brimming your screens,
I am hot kohl eyes:
sultry, on heat with your desire,
hair more black and shiny
than the walls of the Marabar caves,
hair so sheeny polished
that you see your own ecstasy
in its glossed pitch-jet mirror
as my molten body sheathes over you.

Outlaws and desperados know my worth,
but my true sticky-wet itch
is for the good man, the gringo hero.
Only the rounded nodes of a tin star
can scratch me where it satisfies.
The best of the good once licked
my scented honey-salt from his badge:
now he chooses icy Gracie,
frigidaire ad virgin housewife.

I will leave him to his cold blonde bed
and end my days with another lawman,
a builder of dreamboats
who still has to do what a man has to do
no matter the cost to himself.
Now I sit by the river
that will never bear his unfinished craft,
watching him die as his sunset blood
pumps out into a roaring red sky.

It's getting dark, too dark to see, indeed:
but there is still a glimmer and a glint
from the crimson fullness of my lips,
the raven burnish of my glistening hair.
I am Low Midnight before I am High Noon.

Miners of a Different Vein

(Abe Attell v. Harlem Tommy Murphy, March 9th 1912)

They tense their faces from the page,
grime-coated in fine dust blood
like miners from the filthy coal-face.

The Irishman and the Jew
digging rich veins
in the afternoon sun.

Early rounds' bleeding is dried bronze,
sweat-varnished glossy
now the slashing hour is near its end.

Abe's thick black curls stand stiff
as Tommy's crew-crop matts and plasters,
stained leather strains over hammered knuckles.

Set in this sun-bathe circle of men
Abe and Tommy must hack and cleave
till they too may breathe the light.

These miners of a different vein
wield fist-axes fixed in time,
their very wounds freezing the brutal moment.

Not from a common ghetto, yet
united in this seamed blood-bond –
the need to leave this pit alive.

Cloud Pictures

These russet stains on our mattress
are deep embedded rust flowers of our loving.
Your true-blood cycle of crimson being
has been there and gone,
been there and gone,
in affirming, insistent stream.

Now it is at an end,
a release from regular bleeding,
a rhythmic change of pulse.
So for a moment let us celebrate
that which we are asked to ignore,
that which is not discussed.

This has been important to you and me,
your blood has been on our bodies as we loved,
confounding the immaculate deception,
the lie that makes passion anaemic.
Your flush of blood has banished pallour,
defined an earthy heartbeat for our lives.

In recognition of these loving stains,
let us read together the coppered cloud-pictures
transfused for ever beneath where we have lain.

The Westminster Bar, Dawson City:
Old Joanna Hits Her Stride

I must be losing my grip,
all fingers and thumbs
from the nights of white rum.
But the ivory keys draw me in,
rounded at the edges, smoothed,
rancid butter coloured enamel
like the horse-toothed
bar-buttresses I serenade tonight.
I yellow in sallow rhythm-light
to accompany the décor.
Smoking Compulsory Here.
Thank heaven for the black notes,
I cannot tell my chromatic,
rheumatic, tallowed
fingers from the off-whites.
Still, there is a cooling warmth
to the beached bones
of this smoothened keyboard,
salt-scoured by my earthy tunes.
Only my breasts resist
this gorse-hued coarsening,
this mellow tan leathering.
I flaunt a paleness of them tonight
and taunt the limp, curdling drinkers
with my double-barrelhoused,
clotted cream Milk Cow Blues.

There's Nothing There......Is There?

I dipped my head
in the high mountain sky,
and was invited
to stay the night,
to drench my scalp
in small hours indigo,
cryptic counter-code
for day's blazing blue.

And something was there,
heard in slithering scree,
seen in dark shadow-bulks,
scent of pine revealing
a scent not-of-pine,
animal fear on my tongue,
a sense of tense, stealthy touch
deep within.

Azure day's dip
was potent, heady.
Violet night's
was one rational gulp
from drowning.

A Lilliputian in Brobdingnag

Today it is the dust-musty sheaf of magazines
on the lowest shelf in Age Concern
that discloses another new corridor to an old haunt.
The mustard colour-tang of a Lilliput cover
becomes my guide to a familiar ghost-chamber;
the stripling child gripped again
by grainy nakedness and adult words,
the sophistication of the urbane erotic.
Standing there in the shop,
when I come to that story,
the tale I had to read aloud
whilst she dined on me for an hour,
I recognise the familiar lie of the land of the giants.

It is the freshly arriving reminders that startle,
that jolt a bolt-current of flavour to the tongue
when memory peels back to the pith.

Charity was not asking much for this Lilliput.
I thought about buying it,
but I am the grown-up now:
so I said no.

(Lilliput is the name of a magazine that was in print between
1937 and 1960. In its heyday the magazine attracted quality
artists, photographers and writers, but by the late 1950s it had
become a very British form of bourgeois soft porn).

Siberia My Eden

(Lillian Alling Tells Her Story★)

It was the Spring of '25 and the Reds had the Whites on the run,
though I wished a plague on both their slaughterhouses.
Burying my brother's bolshevised body,
Grandfather announced my exile from the steppes –
"The steamer sails from 'vostock within the week,
through Panama and on to the gateway of hope.
I have not kept up my connections with old Kazimir for nothing!
This ticket is the worth and sum of your inheritance,
take it now and make your life in New York,
Kazimir will help you find your feet.
Have your babies in America, my lily,
for our Siberia will soon be an ice-burn on the map,
a mere byword for a sentence of death".
Alone in the last dawn before the 'vostock train
I bathed in the dew of the rich grasses
and crammed the crust of a salt lake into my mouth.
But my attempts at a sick-bed reprieve came to nought,
and soon I was sea-sick swollen in a boilerplate cabin,
home-sick sunstroked on an August-dry New York street.

Old Kazimir helped me find my feet alright –
find my feet as my only true friends!
Professor of Russian Ethnography to the world,
owner of his very own slave drudge to me.
"Oh, my dear, the very structure of your face
reminds me of my beloved Chukchi folk back home!"
I soon found out that his lily liver-spot hands
were more drawn to the contours of my other cheekbones,
so I left him to his dreams and his meanness
and hid for three nights in the New York Public Library,
ghosting my thin frame amongst the steepling stacks
between Russian Languages and Maps of North America.

By side-street tramping and doorstep pleading
I was soon in service, my meagre pay and attic kennel
hard-won rungs above Old Chicken-Neck Chukchi's coop.
I learned the Yankee language fast,
though it might just as well have been Double Dutch,
one babbling voice in New Talk's alien Babel Tower.
My speech, my work, my food and my drink
were all mere means to an end, a heart-quickening desire
to leave that friendless, hateful, teeming ant-mountain.
My soul still sang with the wind in the foxtail barley of the steppes –
I had found my feet, and my precious days away from toil
were spent back among the maps of North America.

Two years to the day from my brother's death
I was on the highway striding west, my long walk underway,
my solitude an invisible banner, no more a shameful secret.
The days, the nights, the weeks, all went by
in the steadiness, the determination of my motion.
Kind folk gave me food and sometimes shelter,
but I refused every offer from every slowing vehicle,
my hands around the short, flattened iron bar,
looted from Old Kazimir's mess of a wine cellar
and rough-sewn into the lining of my jacket.
I might be small and easily overcome,
but there is strength in these Siberian sinews!

Chicago's mazy outskirts taught me to nose north,
and Minneapolis saw to the last leather on my boots.
I still kept up my thirty miles a day,
though my spirits shredded in step with my soles
as I struggled to leave behind my American Dream.
Crossing the border into Canada gladdened my heart
and the kind ladies of Beausejour bathed my sore feet
in the cool waters of Lake Winnipeg,
bought me good boots, fed me real food,
gave me my first friend on that alien continent –

Alice, my wire-curled spring-haunched mongrel.
The nights were better for Alice's need of me.
By day she trotted me through the winds and sun,
the seven hundred miles of plains and farms
to the deep, steepling ramparts of the Rockies,
a beloved barrier to me in their rippling reminders
of the Stanavoy backdrop to my childhood being.

We were coming steadily down the other side
when Alice chased a wolverine, was parted from her throat
with the cleanest of vicious incisions.
I gained Prince George still grieving hard –
I had dreamed Alice racing through purple lupine
after snow-melt on my cherished steppes.
On the Yellowhead west I began to taste the air,
to scent the early Autumn breeze for a salt trace
that might confide ocean to my spying senses,
though my New York Library memories
sent sober images of wilderness, wide rivers,
towering coastal mountains before Pacific glimpse.
From Hazelton I launched my dizzying plan
to strike a necessary north, roadless, without even a trail
for the very first time in all my leg-muscled miles.
But in the books I had learned of a telegraph line
stretching all the way to Fools' Gold land,
Dawson in the come-as-you-are Yukon wilds.

With deep-fresh snows snuggling my calves
I set off to follow the flimsy line on the landscape –
I feared no season, no check, no hurdle, no warnings.
The Gitx'an were kind but my mind was set.
By Second Cabin, just twenty miles out from Hazelton,
I presented a poor, gaunt, weary vision
to Bill Blackstock on his endless maintenance round.
I tried to drive my body on but Bill, my saviour from myself,
tapped back a message to the township

and two days later Hazelton jailhouse was my home.
I would not tell the judge a lie, my legs still moved within my mind,
so he sentenced me to two months in lieu of fine,
and shipped me down to Oakalla Prison, Vancouver's best.
The governor helped me find hotel work to see me through
the wet grey nothing of their feeble Gulf-winter,
and April saw me on the road again,
light-legged, refreshed, impatient, thirsty for steppe-dew.
By July I was back in Hazelton, well welcomed and well warned.
Bill Blackstock organised the telegraph men to aid me
on my journey north, to look out for crazy Russian gals.
By Cabin Eight my body was wracked but my spirit drove on,
buoyed by generous Jimmy Christie's gift,
his precious malamute, one Bruno. Bruno helped me
cross the Nass and many a tortuous mountain pass,
till poisoned bait, a wolf-trap lure, stopped my darling in his tracks
just short of Whitehorse. Here I stonewalled a journalist
and shamefacedly lied about how poor Bruno died.
An icy, snow–bellied Autumn comes early in the north
but I just made Dawson before the wild lands
resumed their 'No Surrender to the Human' pride.

Winter work in hotel and laundry set me up
to buy a wreck, a filthy, battered, hole-hewn hull.
Word soon spread of my soul-sieged plan,
my ultra-urge to reach the gates of my personal Eden
with an ice-melt ride down the serpent Yukon,
sixteen hundred miles to the Alaskan coast
and my first planned human discourse –
a negotiation with some Inuit fisherman, a berth,
a plea to be borne across the Vitus Bering straits.
The toughest, fiercest men from the wild Westminster
all helped to caulk and patch and plug and tar –
though I slipped away on a fresh May dawn
when I heard of the farewells, photos and festive fare.
A Gwich'in hunter found me bewildernessed, lost,

myriad channel paralysed where the Hodzana meets the Yukon.
He showed me Tozi's distant top and set me on my way.
I have never seen such feeling in such impassive features
as when he watched me drift from human sight.
It is there that I shake you off too, curious listener.

My yearning and the empty longing in my gut
become too personal for you to understand my fate,
too much 'For Lillian's Eyes Only' for the world to share in.
Rumour of a woman hauling a small cart towards Teller,
gossip of a Russian woman sleeping rough in Galena Mission,
fanciful lies of weathering storms 'twixt Little and Big Diomede,
even a tale of a woman arriving on a Provideniya beach.
All are futile, sentimental, human happy ending need.
My ballad ends on the bathos of a question mark –
and so it should, for the fibre of my tale is in the telling,
in the minute agonies and the everyday elations of each step,
each single one of my million million paces to my end.
I walk my path still, my restless stride is my summary sufficient,
each step a sliver of now, a momentary action and time
that lasts for ever. I am always at my Eden gate.

(★ This story is my own 'poetic licence' take on the true story of a woman who attempted to walk from New York all the way across Canada in the late 1920s. Her aim was to reach the Alaskan coast and cadge a ride across the Bering Straits, then walk across Siberia back to her home. The best summary of the little that is known about Lillian Alling can be found in Susan Smith-Josephy's Lillian Alling, Caitlin Press, 2011).

I Remember You

You were going to be Bonnie and I was already Clyde,
thief of your heart from some old mouldy vault
in the bank of another. Bereft of running-boards
and smashable windows on a sharp charabanc sedan
with roaring brakes, we stuck our thumbs in the air
to arrive somewhere we could rest our robbers' heads
on each other's kissable, kissed, kissing bellies.
I remember you.
We didn't go down in history, we kept those scars
to ourselves and sewed our secrets into back-seats
of empty cars. I even let you throw knives at me,
knowing you were the only one who shaped me.
I remember you.
We talked in tongues, and you really liked the way
I carried a pink light-bulb for our wayside bedside lamps
just because I loved what it did to your hair, your skin.
I remember you.
We could have died dangerously happy, intertwined,
but you chose a living burial whilst I craved smoke and fire.
Now you've claimed your name again, given me the keys,
the codes, the passwords for another daylight burgling –
And I remember you,
You are still one of us. Still one of Us.

Sheilagh Sparks and Her Flames Sound Like This

"Perhaps my best years are gone…but I wouldn't want them back. Not with the fire in me now." Samuel Beckett, Krapp's Last Tape.

This situation is vacant
as vacant as a vacuous vacancy
in an evacuated vacuum – I am gone
from jobcentre plus
and jobs enter pus
in these boots made for walking
walking away from all great pretending

No more exams no more ex-ams
my ams are not ex my ams are all
extant ecstatic

No more application forms
I lack the application
the applied mathematics
of appliqué on proforma
or on-line format formula one fakery

No job dessications
And no person spifferlications
JDs and person specs and JDs and person specks
and JDs and X-Ray Spex
I'm a germ-free obsolescent
with more essentials
and more desirables
than your sexiest
equal opportunities monitoring form

Fuck my essential criteria
Suck my desirable criteria
Gizza job I could do that!

But I'm striding from the game
with a yellow card from my first referee
and a red from my second referee
and I've always liked red

So I will be poorer
but I will be richer

richer than in the days I sold my self
portrayed myself presented myself
betrayed my self prevented my self
from applying the match
to each shammy scummy scuzzy application
with its o-levels schmo-levels
it's a-levels schmay-levels
o-levels no-levels
a-levels pay-levels
degrees of separation
and masters of none
and bachelors of cup-a-soup
and compliance of science

I will no longer fill
the yawning maw
that is the employment history
or employment mystery
working backwards from the anal now
to the rect…angular boxes
of Cratchitt-coffins
I have inhabited
and dreams I have inhibited
with succinctly succulent sentences
outlining responsibilities
and final salaries and ignoring
the irresponsible attempts
to be human to be humane
and not just watch the paint dry
and the final celery grow
fed by an up-to-date CV
of cosmic vomit
and contestable veracity

Oh freedom from the big fat
empty chunk of sell yourself
in the next bit sell your self
like some sralan-sugar-coated
wannabe win-a-bee wunnerbe
wilderbeest in the china shop
of truth decency and self-respect

No! I shall not be attaching
supplementary sheets no matter how stained

with your juicy reminders to put my name on them
I have had all the learning opportunities
I can possibly learn from
You smoothie earning opportunists
and the gurning opportunities
of your seven-part interview process
will not feature in my life

Nor neither not never not nohow
will consultancy contracts
insultancy-to-the-intelligence con tricks
bleeding the alzheimering arteries
of the public pouch like pubic lice
incisoring away within the budgie-bungling
budget-smuggling speedo greedo
has-been counting big machine

Because if you have a mission statement
you will not have me
you can assume your missionary position
and Invest in People
till the kowtows come home
but you will find that I offer
a very low rate of interest

Poor in pension poor in purse
but so very rich and dripping with freedom
from flogging my soul in your market
the market the mark it out of ten
and don't bother to send her
a sorry not on this occasion letter
because those occasions are gone

Sheilagh is living her life
Living my life I say
without storing up
rather using up my stores
singing out my stories
in this my mess age
my not on message age

Gizza job ad
I could chew that
feed the flames of the fire
that burns with heat and light
so deep within me now."